The
Song
of the
Tree

for
Anja, Timmy
and Arlo

PARTICULAR BOOKS
MMXXI
80 Strand, London

Also by this author
The Fox and the Star
and *The Worm and the Bird.*

The Song of the Tree

Coralie
Bickford-Smith

In the heart of a jungle grew a towering tree.

Every year, when the dry season came,

a flock of birds settled in its branches.

They told the tree of the places they had been.

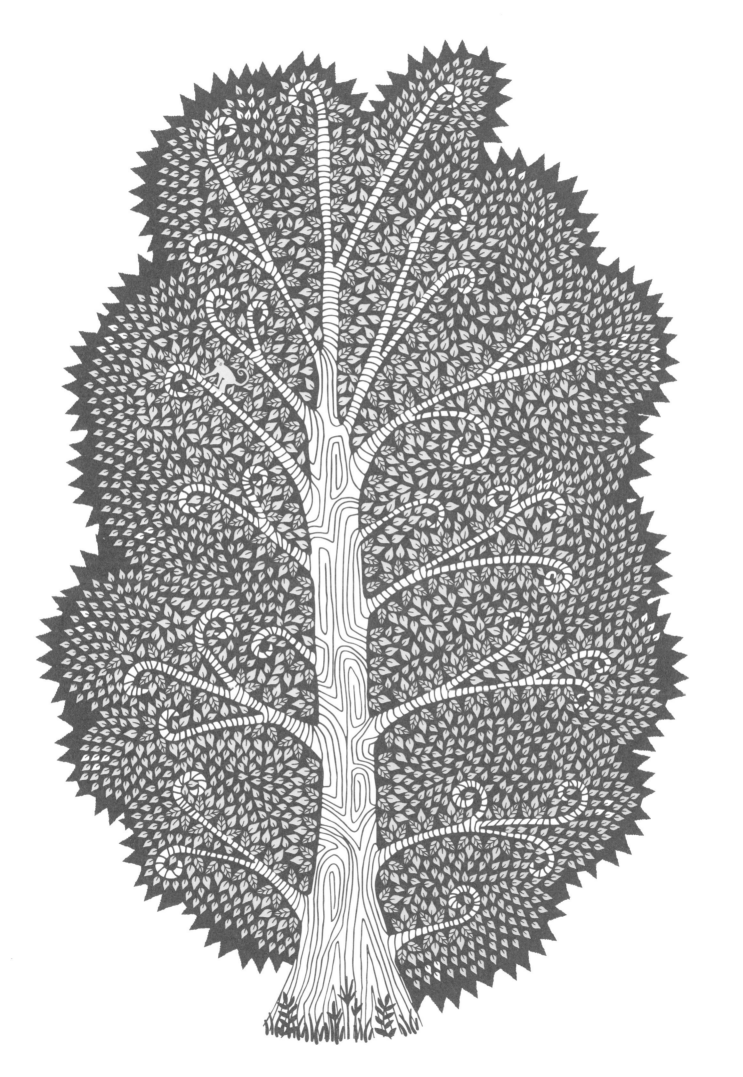

For one
young
bird, this
tree felt
like home,

the
branches
as familiar
as her
own
feathers.

Bird
played idly
in the
tree's lower
thicket.

Her feet dimpled the soft bark with the passing of time.

'I know this tree,
her roots and leaves,

I like this tree,
her peace and calm,

'I love this tree, her steady arms.'

Soon the
rain clouds
gathered
and the flock
began their
parting song.

But Bird was
not ready
to leave
her tree.
She stayed
quiet as the
others sang . . .

'The storms are coming,

the winds carry rain.

It's time to journey,

'it's time for change.
We're off to seek
the sun's warm rays.'

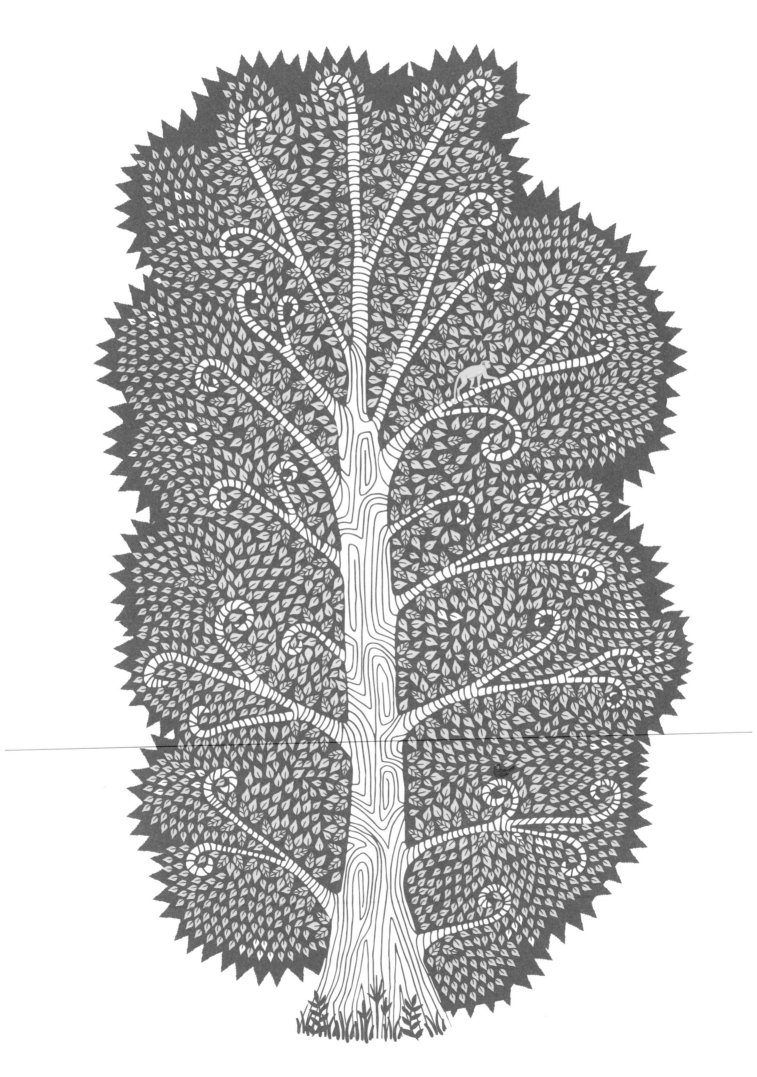

The air began to swell

with the scent of distant lands.

As the flock soared higher,

Bird asked the tree . . .

'When the rains pour down,

who shelters in your branches?

Who rustles your leaves?

Who traces your bark?

Who sings you to sleep?'

Her lone
voice
echoed
through
the gloom.

The tree
sighed.

The jungle
settled.

As
night
time
fell,

the
silence
reached
the
stars.

Brilliant
lights traced
a path up
the tree as
mysterious
notes drifted
through
the air.

'In the blackest night, see our blazing display,

Enchanted
by the
warm glow
of the
fireflies,

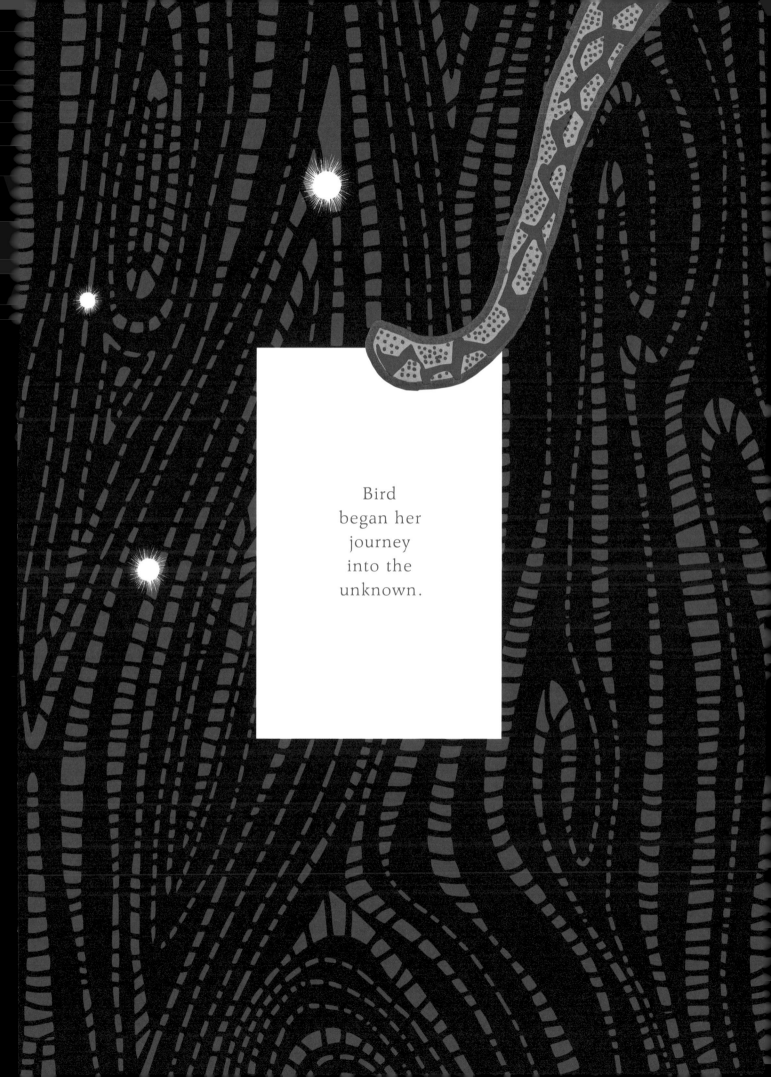

Bird
began her
journey
into the
unknown.

'Our claws are sharp.

Our marks are bright.

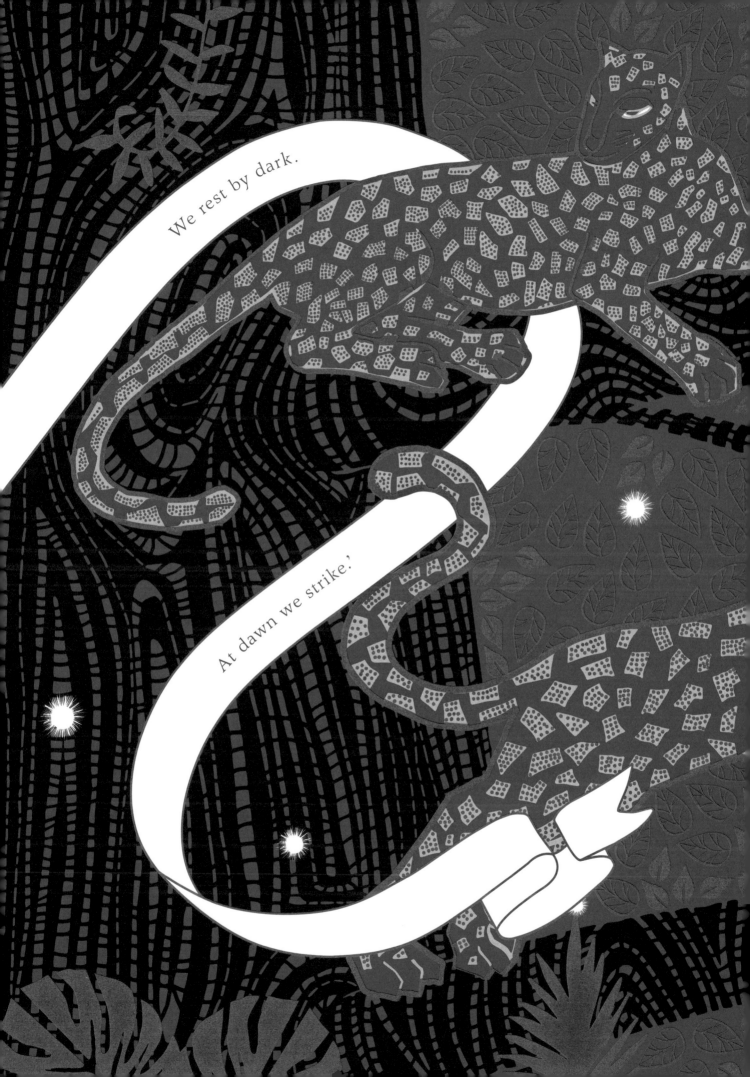

We rest by dark.

At dawn we strike.'

Strange
creatures
surrounded her.

Bird moved
quietly away.

Their rowdy
chorus
receded to
reveal a
single voice.

'No one has feathers

that dazzle like mine,

I preen in the darkness –

tomorrow I'll shine.'

Bird
watched
as a
solitary
leaf began
its long
descent.

All of
a sudden,
leaves flapped,
branches swayed.
The air was
filled with
sound.

'We weave through the branches,

we fly like the wind.

'We jump and we glide, we laugh as we swing.'

Bird
stumbled,
holding
tightly to
the tree.

In the
moonlight
a quiet
voice
began . . .

'I bask in my cloak of colour and light.

You won't find me

by day

or by night.'

As she flew higher

Bird's wings grew light,

the leaves cleared

and the shadows

gave way to

tiny slices

of sky.

'Watch us dance

as we catch

the breeze.

Ready to soar –

we are lighter

than leaves.'

The wind
arrived
rocking
the tree
and teasing
Bird's
feathers.

Urging
her
to
let go,
it sang . . .

'I carry with me every song ever sung.

I float through the trees, I'm here then I'm gone.

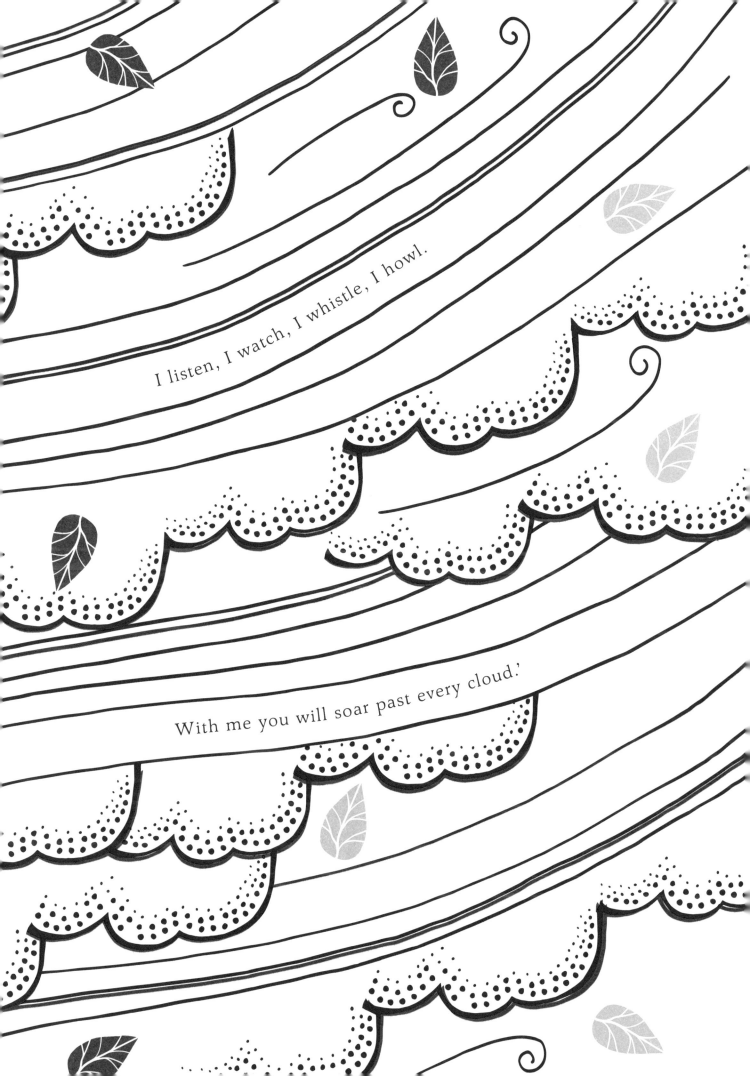

I listen, I watch, I whistle, I howl.

With me you will soar past every cloud.'

Night
dissolved
into dawn.

As Bird
looked out
she was
filled with joy.

She saw
the jungle
anew
and burst
into song.

When the rains pour down

many shelter in your branches.

Many rustle your leaves —

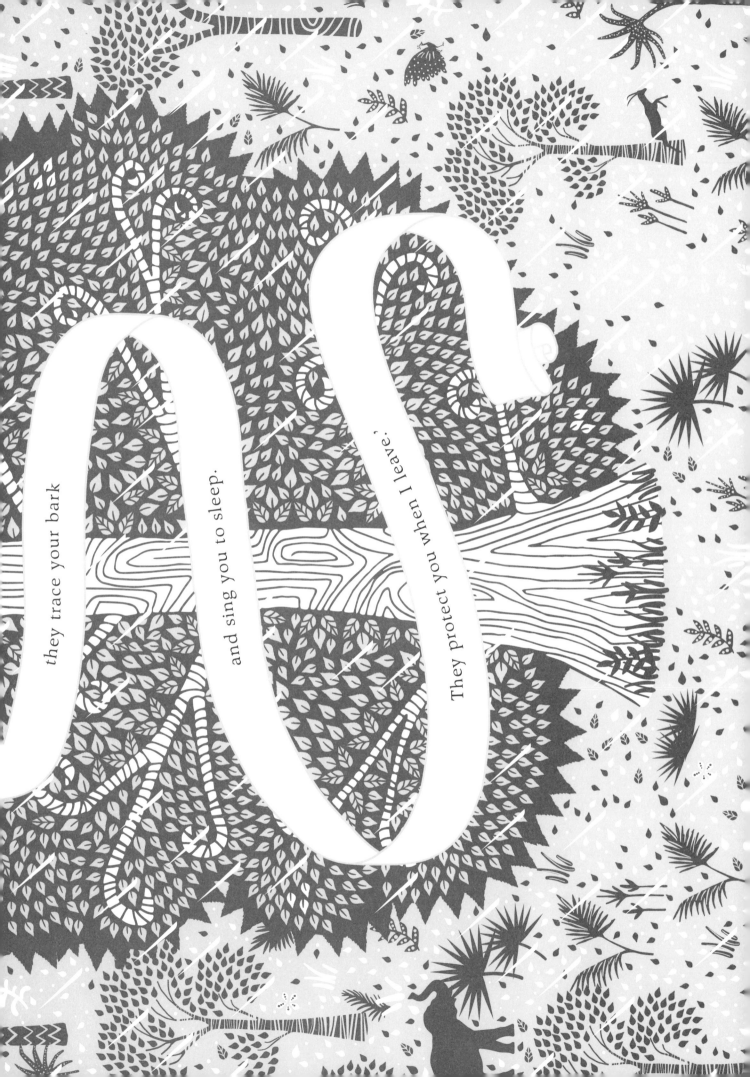

they trace your bark

and sing you to sleep.

They protect you when I leave.'

The Tree creaked.

Bird heard its quiet voice,

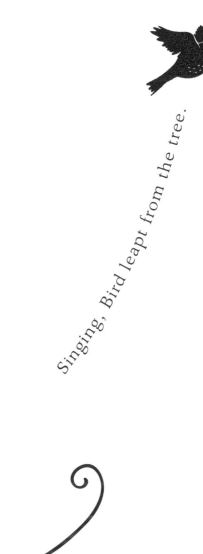

Singing, Bird leapt from the tree.

the whisper of its leaves,

the shifting of its weight.

PENGUIN BOOKS

UK | USA | Canada | Ireland | Australia
India | New Zealand | South Africa

Penguin Books is part of the Penguin Random
House group of companies whose addresses can
be found at global.penguinrandomhouse.com.

First published in Particular Books 2020
Published in Penguin Books 2021
001

Set in Agfa Wile 14.5/18pt
by Coralie Bickford-Smith & Francisca Monteiro
Printed in Italy by L.E.G.O. S.p.A. on Munken Print Cream

A CIP catalogue record for this book is available from the British Library

ISBN: 978–0–141–98934–1

Thank you
C. Stein, H. Conford,
J. Greywoode,
T. Lehman,
J. Stoddart, P. Pawsey,
D. Mackintosh,
and
A. Bickford-Smith.